FUR SHUI™

Ana —
Straight from
my heart to yours!

Patrick Brown

FUR SHUI™

An Introduction to Animal Feng Shui

Written and illustrated by

Paula Brown

The Lyons Press
Guilford, Connecticut
An imprint of The Globe Pequot Press

The Lyons Press is an imprint of The Globe Pequot Press.

Designed and illustrated by Paula Brown

Library of Congress Cataloging-in-Publication Data is available on file.
ISBN 978-1-59921-276-0

Printed in China

10 9 8 7 6 5 4 3 2 1

Contents

Furr
Shui
Purr
Shui
Purr
Furword: The Black "Cat" School of Feng Shui

Everything is made of energy and energy has its home in all your spaces, places, and being. Feng shui is a very ancient and popular practice that entices healthy flow of chi (energy) in one's home, business, environment, and even within one's body. After much study of Black Hat Feng Shui, I have found that both intent and attention to what and where items are placed in one's environment makes an immediate impact on one's life and home. When I get stuck in any of life's aspects I take a look around my space (both physical *and* mental) and apply feng shui principles to get the situation running more smoothly. Energy moves the way you guide it to move. It works!

My profession as an animal communicator (and using energy movement for healing and soothing my clients) has naturally made me aware of gathering tools that could help me and my clients understand and help their furry partners. It has made sense to always ask about an animal's environment, both physical and emotional, to find solutions to the challenges my people and fur clients bring to my awareness. Animals bring so much loving energy into your life. Most of my animal clients express their need to help with their person's health, abundance, and relationships. They are powerful healers, curling up to your heart center when you are blue. Fur friends are great at their jobs as guards; standing by your front door (of your home *and* heart) protecting and guarding your life paths, relationships, and belongings. Many act as muses of your inspiration for your creativity and expressions of love. They are pretty intuitive (I find much more than us humans!) on how to move chi around, doing this naturally to enhance their health and even *your* health and space.

All "fur beings" are governed by the flow of chi in and out of their environment and bodies. Believe it or not, they have the same energy and movement of energy in themselves and their space, just as we do in ours.

With this acknowledgment of fur chi, welcome to a new expression of Black Hat Feng Shui: the Black Cat School of Fur Shui! Cover to cover this primer not only points out auspicious Black Hat Feng Shui principles, but also reflects in *itself* the laws of feng shui in the use of color (black for career, red for fame, the guas explained with their specific colors), design (a balance of restful and active space with your guide, the Black Cat

7

guarding and protecting its pages) and even the total page number of 101—finishing the fundamentals of Fur Shui-101. The Black Cat School carefully "walks its talk."

Our animal friends (both domestic and wild) can really boost and enhance our positive energies in harmony with career, health, family, relationships, creativity, skills, fame, travel, and helpful people (coincidentally all the sectors of the feng shui bagua!) *if* we know how to encourage their energies and well-being. On the other hand, if we misuse or abuse their being, health, and happiness, we are stealing not only their positive energies, but ours as well. So be careful, pay attention; knowing how to boost and support their energies will give you a great flow of chi, giving all aspects of your lives together the greater lessons of quality of life, precious fun, and joyous love.

It is finally time to take a look at how their and your environment are working or co-existing in good and not so good manners. This is a fun primer, just a brief beginning at taking a good look at how to get some healing chi to work for you and your animal friends. So, why not apply this proven method of feng shui, or energy coercion, to one's special purr or fur ball? Hence a wonderful new world of Fur Shui!

Get going and get creative with *Fur Shui*. In the following pages you can take a look and get a few ideas at how this auspicious practice of Black Hat Feng Shui easily translates into Black Cat Fur Shui.

This is merely a fun guide to get you thinking and possibly moving some fur chi about. See how you and your animal can benefit from the powers of Fur Shui, have fun, and start moving some positive energy into any situation in your home and life!

A note from my wise mentor and Black Hat Feng Shui master, Nate Batoon, of the Hawaiian Tibetan School of Black Hat Feng Shui:

"What a wonderful book! In my some sixteen years as a feng shui consultant, I have met many delightful animals that not only bring to their owners the love, fun, and comfort that we are familiar with, but also great chi for feng shui. This great book brings this awareness—your furry and nonfurry friends can help with the feng shui of your home!

I am glad that Paula has written this book to honor our furry friends and to give us practical and powerful feng shui tips—in short Black Cat Fur Shui is purrrrr-fect."

Nate Batoon
Feng Shui Master

Feng Shui Masters Disguised as Animals

Hot chi dogs, black hat cats, our furry, feathered, sometimes scale-covered, sometimes finned, two- to four-legged friends are all a menagerie of chi masters we call pets.

The Chinese have defined our life force energy as chi. Everything has it and it is proper and good to keep it flowing and healthy at all times. Animals not only make great companions, they also enhance the flow of chi into one's home and life.

Chirping Chi

Pets sing, talk, snooze, play, and move about, *and* along with them so does chi! Those rugs, shoes, or various clothing favorites our animals fetch, knead, rearrange or simply insist upon owning are packed with their magical energy— their chi. Our animal friends are the movers and shakers not only of their chi, but of our home's chi. They have a nose for where the good chi is, sniffing it out in our slippers, gowns, and favorite tees.

Dogs sniffing, cats purring, birds chirping— they sing our songs and are on a mission to wrangle our attention to get a bit of our energy for a warm hug, loving stroke, or special treat. All are clever keepers and movers of chi, both in our hearts and homes.

Defining Fur Shui

Water

Feng shui is Chinese for "wind" and "water." Just the right combo of the two energies creates a harmonious balance in our world. Symbolic of the balance of energies found in nature, our animal friends find their own expression of balance in their own homes and health. So be sure the next time you wash your pet he does not fly away like the wind!

Wind

Animals can make a home a joyous, active, positive place if they indeed are loved and happy. On the other hand, if they are ignored or not kept healthy and happy, a person's home and life will experience negative energy flow.

By using the basic knowledge of feng shui and applying it to your pet's life and home you can certainly help keep the chi moving and growing! Continue on and discover the importance of Fur Shui . . .

It's a Balancing Act

Fur Balance = Fur Yin / Fur Yang

Yin is at rest, yang is in activity.

Yin and Yang Attraction

A balance of both gives one peace and deep contentment. Yin is the feminine, patient, and nurturing intuitive essence, and yang is the masculine, more physically active, and aggressive trait. A happy and healthy animal exists when equal parts of yin and yang are present. When balanced, your pets are not only attractive to you, they are attractive and socially popular with other animals. A true party animal is created!

Playing, walking, running, or exercising with your furry friends and then giving them comfy places to rest make for a happy home and pet.

Animals can help bring you and your house into balance (as with balanced activities of exercise, rest, and play), bringing harmonious energies to your life. They offer you warm cuddle opportunities after long hectic days and give loving licks and pamperings to other furry friends within your family. Balance is the key to their good health and happiness as well as blessing you with the same.

An equal part of active energy and at-rest energy can be seen in a healthy animal.

As moving objects energize a space, animals moving about bring chi into areas of your home and life. With their physical movement throughout our homes, their habit of playing and exercising can bring great energy and happiness to their life and your home.

Harmonious Energies

17

Fur Chi Wiz!

Chi is what we know and call energy. It is the invisible force that keeps the world as we see it working and in place. Everything is made of chi. Without chi, nothing would exist; it is what makes atoms move, rocks stay still, and a cat's deep purr travel through the air to be heard by you and me.

Animals attract chi; they seem to be natural magnets for chi movement and flow. They also have built-in radar for good chi areas. Your furry folk occupy and are attracted to the "good feeling" places as well as heal areas that need their loving and positive energy. Just look at where they like to rest, the items they are attracted to, or their favorite places, and you will find where the restorative things and peaceful spots are in and around your home (as well as some spots that could benefit from some chi movement!).

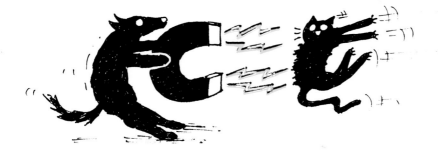

Moving Chi

The Fur Bagua

The bagua is an octagon (called the "ba") whose shape and interior divisions define the nine categories of life (each category is called a "gua"). There are nine "life areas" affecting your home and your animal's environment. This bagua is a visual map of these spaces in your home and throughout your world. In the home, your whole house plan can be placed under the bagua's structure and each room can have its own bagua designation. You just use the "entrance" or front of each space as the area to begin, with the black portion (career) placed at the entrance. Wherever you go, you can place this invisible "map" in rooms, cars, parks, restaurants, cities, even where your helpful people are: the vet, doggie and kitty day care, and animal groomers!

The nine life areas include career, helpful people and travel, creativity and children, relationships and love, fame and reputation, prosperity, family, skills and knowledge, and finally health. The bagua's eight sides and center form a container for placement of the areas, and this symbol is usually applied to your living area (single rooms, whole house area, and also your yard) with the career side at the bottom, which is placed at your doorway. (Wherever you go, place the career section always at the entrance or front of your location.) Take a look at the bagua for this ancient Chinese configuration and locate the guas in your home.

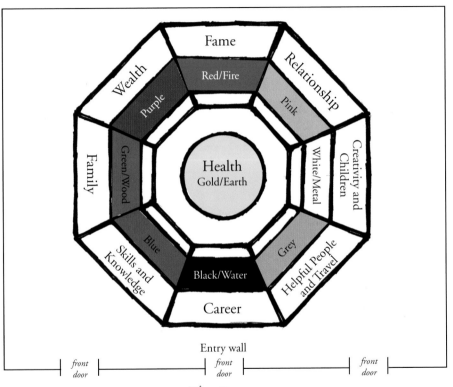

The Bagua
(Fur and Nonfurry)

Let the Fire Chi Reign

Is there a place (now referred to as a gua) in your home (let's face it, it is really your animal's home!) you would like to amp up for yourself or your furry friend? Is an animal already doing its energy "job" for you? Or . . . is there a part of your life or their life—relationship, health, family (they all need buddies, too!)—where some energy is needed? Animals are a natural energy booster; they gravitate to where the energy feels the strongest and most comfortable. Where do they like to sleep (are they building up your "fire" energy in your fame section or are they hogging all your loving energies in the relationship area? Wherever you need their energy, make them comfortable. Amazingly enough animals already have their job assignments in your life and they need you to accordingly amp up their chi or energy to do their job well. All animals have professions, jobs, and purposes for their life and your life. That's where color and placement come in for you both. Just look at the next few pages for a start on how to identify, augment, and magnify furry energy qualities in any gua or corner of your heart or theirs.

Fur Shui Alert!   *Be sure to remember to put your intent of what you want the situation to bear into the space, object, thought, or form that you want to increase the flow of chi. Thought and positive intent is a *must* to activate the flow of chi in any situation, furry or nonfurry!

Gleaming Chi! *(A Few Things to Know Before You Get to Know the Guas!)*

Every shape, sound, object, color, smell, and symbol in a place, room, or space affects the chi for that space or person or fur friend that goes in and out of that space. Remember: Keep it all clean for good clean fun and flowing chi!

Most obviously, your furry friend needs to always smell and look bright and fresh. A dirty furry friend in any way is a big stop sign for healthy chi in any gua he occupies. Plus, this is just downright unpleasant for both of you. Healthy ears and teeth are clean and fresh. Get your friend checked out and maintained from nose to furry fanny to keep the chi he fires up healthy and moving. Nothing like a shiny smile and fresh breath for him to attract both furry and nonfurry friends!

Keep that fish bowl in your career gua fresh and clean and see how happy and well your fish friends will be. Ick on the fish means ick in the bowl means ick in your career!

Happiness Is Fresh "Flipper" Chi

Fur Chi Dos and Don'ts

Eating spaces are especially important for your furry friends. Dirty, cluttered, unkempt, smelly food bowls and unclean water dishes only attract "dis-ease" for you and your animals. In other words, bad chi! When the food is fresh, bowls and surrounding areas kept clean with bowls full of fresh water alongside your four-legged friends are happy and healthy. Your hard work keeping this area clean results in good health for everyone, making the chi running through this area happy and supportive. If this area is a literal "fly zone," then clean up quickly; take away that buggy landing strip ASAP!

The Bagua Areas:

Outlining the many qualities and characteristics of Fur Chi

The basic keys for understanding each gua in the fur bagua.

Gua	Color	Element	Number	Shape
Life Path/Career	Black	Water	6	Irregular, undulating, free form (not sharp and pointy, square and rectangular, but soft and rounded)
Helpful People/Travel	Gray	None	5	Anything that pleases you
Children/Creativity	White (creativity combines *all* the colors into one!)	Metal	3	Round, mounded shapes
Love/Relationships	Pink, red, and white (can have a bit of gold as accents)	None	2	Any shape is OK (soft and round is "huggy")
Fame/Reputation	Red	Fire	1	Pointed shapes, triangular

Gua	Color	Element	Number	Shape
Wealth/Prosperity	Purple, gold, blue-red, green, red	None	8	Any shape goes, maybe a "$" shape?
Family/Elders/ Community	Green	Wood	4	Rectangular, vertical, columnar
Skills/Knowledge	Blue, green, black	None	7	Shapes are defined by your own tastes and skills
Health/Balance	Yellow/earth hues	Earth	9	Square, flat, horizontal

Fur Shui Is a Balanced Composition

27

Unlocking the Treasures of Fur Shui

Now we go into the places and spaces housing all that Fur Chi. A Black Cat fur tour of the bagua and all of its guas!

Fur-Filled Purpose

Your soul/life/career path is represented in this space of the bagua. Believe it or not, your animal *also* has a soul/life path and comes into your life with its "job," so to speak! Rescue dogs, kitty cat food stars, stunt birds, and also those trained Willards out there all get their chi from this gua. The firehouse Dalmatians and the "shop" cats and dogs you see as you do your errands all have their jobs and need to be comfortable and confident in what they do and how they serve. Your friend's job could also be that important support of your happiness and joy, your source of play and fun! Could be that your animal is a wise monklike being whose job is to not only guide you, but also show you the depth of your soul.

There is also the possibility that your animals show you and help you with *your* job. They help you keep your eye on the prize by supporting you daily with love, understanding, and loyalty. Think of all the times you have spent burning the midnight oil with them by your side and also reminding you that it is time to take a couple of stretch breaks, snacks and meals? Taking a breather now and then has inspired some pretty fine ideas.

You can strengthen this section or place in your home by simply being very trendy with the color black. Place a moving fun sculpture or mobile (how about a cow jumping over the moon?), moving water feature, or perhaps Fido's extra water dish (this area is *all* about water and *flow*) just outside the front door.

This, according to Eastern philosophy, is a great place to keep a fish. A healthy fish and a clean fishbowl attract not only chi, but also loads of prosperity and good luck. Just watch it swim and move about in its round bowl (tempting that kitty of yours) while bringing in strong water energy into your home and animals. Hey, cat and fish can be an auspicious combo when both are in harmony. Even if your cat's job is to be a wise old monk soul, take care, this could be a destructive cycle also. Just keep your fishbowl outside of paw reach.

Black Cat Says: Honor Your Life Path

ommmmmmmmmmmm . . .

Helpful People/Travel:

Want to find the perfect helpers for you and your fur friend? Then pay attention to this section. Your animal friends can be your best helpers. They fetch your paper or slippers, give you love and attention when you need it most by purring, offering you a paw, and always giving you moral support and unconditional love. Service dogs are famous helpers for many in need! Why not clear out this area in your home and support those that support you with some added gray tones, some silver accents, and maybe a photo of one of your helpful people/animals or angels?

Ease of travel is also in this gua. If you have the space, why not store your furry friend's travel bed or carrier here? It is sure to attract all sorts of divine chi and assistance for your next outing. Here's the spot to put your pup's leash or harness handily hanging and ready for some use and fun. You can ask for help here and get support for your travels, receiving smooth passage and angelic guidance!

Rover loves to ride in the car . . . or maybe not? The travel gua in your auto is the passenger seat right beside the driver's seat, so unless your dog chooses to drive, a good spot is right beside you, safely strapped in and comfy in his or her travel bed. (Watch out, the backseat of your SUV is the career section where serious play can magnify; a favorite spot for two furry folk whose life path purpose is to cavort!)

Always Go the Chi Limit!

Children/Creativity:

Laughter is the best medicine, so let's all be creative, playful kids again! Most of the time our animal friends can be pretty creative and loads of fun. This is the spot for the toy chest. Your fur ball just loves to bat around those sparkle balls, catnip mice, feather wands, tin balls, and just about anything that rolls. The kitty climbing towers are great here as well as all those toys you bought for man's best friend, be it a cat, dog, bird, or hamster. This would be a great place for a hamster Habitrail™—just watch them race! And what about that electric train or miniature car racetrack? The "Attack of the Giant Cat" or "The Humongous Playful Paw" comes into play with all sorts of moving objects that can hang in this area.

Expecting a litter of pups or kitties? (Best to keep the hot-to-trot bunny couples out of here . . . way toooo creative!) Maybe this would be a great space for the nest and nursery for the little ones after they come into the world. Support for creation and children are here when the gua's requirements of something metal, white, and toylike are placed in this space. A nice round metal bowl with sparkling clear water along with a metal food dish for some snacks would be purrrrfect. Soft mounds of sheepskin pillows or bedding could intensify your animal's energy and comfort here. Play hard, eat hard, rest well!

Master of Fur Shui Play

Love/Relationships:

Love, love, love . . . love is all you need (Wasn't that the song of some pretty famous bugs?). Relationships can be blissful or not so! Is the warm snoozing animal on your bed in sync with your dreams and midnight snacks? Or are your furry friends crowding you out of your own bed? If so, why not try to give them a soft comfy bed in the far right corner of the room . . . that's the love/relationships corner that could benefit from their loving vibes and loyalty. Or if you have two or more furry friends, put all their beds in the right corner space of your home so they can all send love into your home and be supported by the love they have for each other. It's like Noah's Ark; this is the story of two by two. Just see what happens if two bunnies are in this corner . . . you soon have many loving souls to bless your home. Any combo of two loving furry things is great.

You can take your dog out for a walk and check out and attract some possible romantic partners (for either him *or* you!), why not use a pink leash or pink collar? Hey, even you guys, pink does attract some pretty fine females for you and your pooch! And what's more lovable (for female *or* male) than a cute, cuddly dog friend?

Eastern philosophy states that a pair of mandarin ducks is good luck when placed in your relationship area (southwest corner of your home or room). Although ducks would be

True Love Fur Sure!

great to have as pets, maybe a painting or a carved set would fulfill this good luck for you more than the living set! A nice purring cat pair or loving puppy snuggled into this space can bring loving chi into your romance sector.

Fur Shui Alert! *Classic feng shui also warns against placing fish and frogs in this area. So, let's keep it only warm and fuzzy here for all!

Fame/Reputation:

Fame, fortune, and recognition are what most of us desire. So do lots of our animal friends. Trigger, Lassie, Seabiscuit, Felix the Cat, and Mr. Ed all have claimed their fame and our hearts. Your fame section in the home is straight across from your entrance and career section. This makes total sense! Your animal has a job, and it claims its recognition from that job, be it well done or not so well done! Animals also hold Fire energy that is compatible with the element found in the Fame gua. Place a nice red bed in this area of your home and energize and support your fame section with your animals' warm fire energies. Great place for a kitty gym and sleep tent. Have a dog or cat that has a bit of low energy or lack of confidence? Put a red snappy collar on him and see if this gets more compliments, energy, and recognition while on walks. You love Lassie and want to get your pooch into the limelight? Then dress up your fame section in your home with photos of that canine hero along with your dog's soon-to-be famous mug.

Have a horse you ride, show, and place in competition? Put his ribbons and future blue and purple ribbons along this wall and boost their fame and fortune and yours. (A nice red accent in the harness would be a great energy activator also.)

Fur Shui Alert! *NEVER put your animal's—dog, kitty, bird—water dish in the fame section. You are pouring their H_2O on your and their fame's fire!

"Chi-Struck"

Wealth/Prosperity:

Money, wealth, abundance, prosperity, anyway you say it, we all deserve wealth in every aspect of our lives. Animals give you an abundance of love, play, laughs, and inspirations in all areas of your life. Given unconditionally too! So, why not give some rewards to your friends who help you through balancing checkbooks, listening to your worries, and helping you celebrate your triumphs. Maybe a treat jar for your dog or cat (organic food snacks, catnip, special toys) can go in this area of your home or room. Put these treats in a magnificent purple jar and reward them generously. This northwest corner of your home or room needs to have all sorts of "rewards"(including extra warm petting and compliments) in it. The gua's color is royal purple, which can also be touched with gold (gold coins too!). Why not a neat, deep purple pet blanket or purple collar and leash? Want some money to come into your life, deck out that dog with purple; hats, coats, collars, toys all are royal treats for you and them. Remember, animals are chi magnets, let the abundance doors open with their loving and unconditional energy.

The Chinese say that this is also the place (north corner of home) that keeping a pet turtle would be very auspicious; *only* in the living or dining rooms, please, never in the bath or kitchen. For good luck, turtles are tops! They bring luck into your life and symbolize protection in households. Just give them a home in a ceramic pot or container at least eighteen inches in diameter, half filled with water with a rock island in the middle. They need a choice of being in or out of the water (I'm talking about the small guys that are typically found in pet stores and not dessert or turtle folks found in the wild) along with a diet full of fresh green veggies, fish food, and some nice words of love and thanks. No need for more than one. Turtles are notorious loners and will not be at all in need of many turtle friends.

Your animals provide you with abundant love and happiness, why not put their photo in this gua area to support and strengthen their own joyous prosperity.

Attract a Fur-tune!

Family/Elders/Community:

We are all part of one big happy family! With this section of the bagua, family of all sorts is represented. Your furry friend is just as much a part of your family as all of your human children or siblings. Seeing that many birds such as parrots live into their sixties, they also are remembered in wills, legacies, and inheritances. Be careful, maybe Fido will inherit the family estate because of his greater loyalty to your patron. Take a tip from your loyal furry friends, strengthen your connection to family and community and you will benefit greatly in both love and respect.

This is where your animals can really teach you so very much. A litter of pups to a hutch full of bunnies, all are taken care of unconditionally by mom and dad as well as the occasional orphan who is lovingly adopted by a big-hearted animal mom. Mom dogs have been known to nurse orphaned kittens. And then there's always the story of Tarzan, rescued and raised by the apes!

Why not put your new puppy's or kitten's bed with ticking clock (mom's heartbeat) in this gua until he fully becomes part of your human family? Your pet will feel love, support, and comfort in this area, and you just may get some sleep at night also! A nice green, rectangular-shaped soft bed would be just the perfect thing. Put some photos of your family (which of course includes your furry friends!) and friends in this area of

Fur Family Chi

your home to remind you just how important family is to your life. Both past and present family remembrances belong here. The ID name tag from your first pet that may not be here with you now, photos, pet family trees, and all those "gifts" from your animal friends can be placed in this section. Maybe you have a favorite toy you and your friend play with during your quality-with-Rover time? This is just the spot to keep these treasures.

This is a great place for the kitty condo and clawing "family tree." Get that cat family chi strong and working for you and them every day.

Skills/Knowledge:

Think you know *so* much about your furry friends? Well, that's not half of what they really know about you! They know things before you speak them because they listen to your heart. Let's all learn more about them in our skills and knowledge gua or place in our home. Bring out those books on raw food diets, Chinese medicine and herbs, holistic healings, and tales of heroics, deep loyalty, and love from and for animals. Get reading and learn a few things to make you and your furry friend even more content! This is a good area to place books and videos on everything from horsemanship to how to clip your cat's claws.

Practice makes perfect, and this is a great place to teach those tricks to Fido or Felix the cat. Fetch, sit, roll over, spin like a top, smile, whatever makes you both accomplished, happy, and skillful!

Putting in the time to both participate and generate wisdom in this gua will certainly pay off, keeping you and your animal up to date, competitive, successful, and wise. (This is the owl's corner for sure. If you have one as a pet, this is his home roost! If not, a photo of the wise owl works just fine also.) Knowing what to do and when to do it is what this gua is all about!

Fetching Fur Shui Skills!

You have an agility or Frisbee dog? Then why not give him or her a nice blue kerchief or collar to keep the dog's skills honed and brilliant! A horse that is a hunter/jumper, dressage, or arena competitor? Makes sense to add a bit of blue under the saddle or in the harness or reigns. The skills are also yours, so why not add a bit of blue to your outfit to help you remember all those commands and responses? Why do you think the prized number one ribbon so often is blue? Skills and knowledge when used brilliantly and balanced nets you some fine blue number ones. Put your rewards and ribbons in this section of your home. In your horse's home or stall, this area is the left corner close to the stall entrance. Deck it out with the blue ribbons you strive for or have already won. Recognize and support your and your furry friend's accomplishment!

Health/Balance:

Last but not least is the ninth gua, which is in the center of all the guas: health! This gua holds the centered chi of health we all need in order to actualize all the other guas. No health, no nothing! This is where laughter could just be the best medicine, which we are provided much of by our furry friends. Think of all the funny things and smiles they give to us. Feeling down? Just take your dog for a walk, your cat for a petting purr test drive, or listen to the cooing of your bird as it gives you sweet bird kisses and bounces up and down on its perch. We want our animals to be happy and healthy!

Yellow/gold is the color in this section. Just like the cheerful face of the sunflower turning to look at us from the garden! Give your animals yellow fuzzy toys, brilliant gold sparkle balls, along with your own warm laughter and smile. That yellow Frisbee you toss for your dog is keeping him and you both full of health and well-being.

Unbalanced Claw Chi

Keep their and your dispositions bright by strengthening this section of your home with earth tones, square shapes, and flat, horizontal objects. Perhaps a few nice flat chew toys for Rover can be given in the health gua to keep teeth clean and healthy? Maybe your kitties' flat cardboard scratching box can live here to get those muscles flexed, stretched, and in shape. Giving your kitty this Fur Shui tool here will certainly keep that nice gold-toned easy chair in fine shape and *not* become the favorite kitty clawing spot!

The hamster Habitrail™ can be wonderful here with its yellow tube passageways creating all sorts of exercise opportunities for the 'sters. Have a hamster or pet mouse? Then put its exercise wheel right in the middle of the cage and watch the little one go like crazy while staying in shape.

Put a picture of your friend all happy and healthy in a gold or yellow frame adding his name with a personally composed love wish and message for good health and harmony on the photo's back.

A good thing to do for your animals' health is to give them a healthy diet too. A yellow square food dish and water combo would cheer up your pets' eating area as well as cheer up their tummies. Just put the absolute best stuff for them in their bowls (take a look at the Skills and Knowledge info on pp. 44–45)!

Unbalanced Winded Chi

Balanced Win-Win Chi

This is the balance area of the gua where yin and yang are in perfect harmony. So, why not put a cuddle spot right in the center if you can for your animals to relax, refresh, refuel with each other. The color here is earth tones and the shape is square for the cushions.

The five guas that hold the five elements and their colors.

There are five guas that are anchored by elements that make up the earth. Fire, metal, water, wood, earth all make up everything we see or use every day. These elements are the dictators of positive and constructive cycles (examples given after the next few element pages), harmony or disharmony in your house and life. Items that represent each element are made of that element (its amount and form are important) or the actual element can be represented by assigned shapes or color. So balance the elements for your home and fur partners and you will have much Fur Shui success!

*Grounded Earthly Chi Muncher
(Original Earth Chi Recycler)*

The Fur Shui Elemental Chart

Gua	Color / Shape	Element	Results
Life Path/Career	Black Irregular,	Water	Black is solid success (being in the black), insight, Undulating depth (like the ocean), mysterious and single-minded; in solitude.
Children/Creativity	White Round, Mounded Shapes	Metal	White is formed and forged by combining all the colors and represents purity, innocence, spirituality, creation (rainbows all come from white light).
Fame/Reputation	Red Pointed Shapes, Triangular	Fire	Red says "fire," it is a catalyst ("light my fire"), stimulating good fortune, success, prosperity, and joy.
Family/Elders/ Community	Green Rectangular, Vertical, Columnar	Wood	Green is nature's nurturing color (go "Green," support Mother Nature) that brings you fresh new life in the spring, new beginnings, abundance of growth, prosperity, and health.
Health/Balance	Yellow/Earth Hues Square, Flat, Horizontal	Earth	Yellow brings you good cheer (smiley sun face), patience, and clarity as well as joy and good health.

Water/Life Path/Career:

Water is the element of the entranceway to your home and career gua. Deep, clean water is the home of many colorful fish, fresh- and saltwater. Put a simple goldfish or an exotic carp pond in this space. Give the fish a castle, clean H_2O, good food, nice plants, and they will attract abundance and energy into your career, life path, and home. This is also the place that Fido likes to shake off after a walk in the rain! This is a good thing, just duck (*they* are welcome here also) and avoid the free shower.

Metal/Children/Creativity:

Get creative with the metal element. Birds in gilded cages would be grand in this gua. Metal food and water bowls go here also. Those metal training clickers get immediate response here along with fluffy white toys and beds for your furry friends.

Too much metal may be dangerous when used in choke collars and chains. Excess in any element is not good. Why not follow your dog's natural creative instincts and be pulled into the fire hydrant magnetic zone. Lots of friendships are "sniffed out" and formed at the hydrant.

Too Much Metal Element

Fire/Fame/Reputation:

Where's the fire? It should be in your fame gua along with your animal's bright red cushion. As mentioned before, animals carry natural fire energy and they naturally pump up your fame section when encouraged to rest and hang out there. Give them a big OK and encouragement just to be in this space. Furry folk are famous for their fire chi, so let them stir the flames of your success!

Wood/Family/Elders/Community:

Would a woodchuck chuck wood if a woodchuck could chuck wood? Who knows! But you need some strong wood energy in your family gua for sure. And, Rover loves to fetch and sometimes chuck about with his favorite stick or two. Now, stick throwing is not commonly accepted in a home so we have to take other measures in this gua ("Take it outside the gua," your mom would say). Maybe you let Rover chew on his favorite prize stick here or give him a substitute chew toy that is brown and sticklike? For a cat, a nice clawing post or climbing tree would be just right.

Earth/Health/All Other Cases for Balance and Harmony:

Earth, outside it is OK (well, maybe) for a doggy digging project, but why not bring the earth inside with a container of kitty grass for munchies along with a pet rock perhaps? Perfect examples of a good, healthy Fur Shui earth element are the yummy hay and alfalfa treats that your horse loves (keep that alfalfa in balance and movin' with some good pounding *on* the earth exercise). Outside activities involving sand boxes, bone burials, and dirt baths all seem more appropriate for your furry friends. All of this good earth energy outside adds to your property and your pet's good vibe as well as purely inside activities!

Fur Shui "Gold Strike" in Mother Earth

Fur Your Comfort. It's All Elemental!

Are you and your animal finding comfort with the elements?

Each gua that holds an element in the Fur Shui bagua can have (already existing or added on) elemental characteristics and items inside that gua, which can either build up or erode the gua's native element. Complementary elements, items, shapes, or activities that strengthen a gua or section of your life are considered to be creative or constructive items that create what we call constructive cycles. Elements, items, shapes, and activities that are opposite to or contrary with the elemental personality of the gua when brought into that gua will weaken the gua's native element and then becomes a destructive force or destructive cycle to the gua. The big question is: Are you and your furry friends finding ultimate comfort or discomfort in each elemental gua, in balance with the gua's natural elements? Just what complements an element and what does not? Turn the page to recognize and discover a few useful furry elemental facts. Then, use your imagination and come up with some fun constructive elemental Fur Shui cycles that can benefit you, your home, and your fur friends.

A quick explanation of elemental creative or constructive cycles would be: starting at the career gua element and going clockwise around the bagua, water feeds wood (family), wood feeds fire (fame), fire produces earth (health), earth makes metal (creativity), metal holds water (back to career) So, all elements when paired up in this manner are in the flow of creating and supporting.

On the Fur Shui bagua elemental wheel, opposites do not attract, they weaken! Look at the bagua and see how the combination of elements affects each other. Simple elemental weakening or destructive cycle combinations: water with fire drowns fire's flames, fire with metal melts away the metal, metal with wood cuts down the wood, wood with earth stabs into the earth, and earth with water dams up the water or just plain makes mud. These combos weaken each gua, and things may just get a bit confused or blocked.

Look at the chart on the next page for a few basic clues to become element-friendly.

THE FUR SHUI CREATION AND DESTRUCTION CYCLES CHART

Gua	Element	Cycles
Life Path/Career	Water	Creation cycle items: metal, white, round
		Destruction cycle items: earth, yellow, square or horizontal
Family/Elders/Community	Wood	Creation cycle items: water, black, undulating
		Destruction cycle items: metal, white, round
Fame/Reputation	Fire	Creation cycle items: wood, green, rectangular, or columnar
		Destruction cycle items: water, black, undulating
Health/Balance	Earth	Creation cycle items: fire, red, pointed
		Destruction cycle items: wood, green, columnar, or vertical
Children/Creativity	Metal	Creation cycle items: earth, yellow, square, or horizontal
		Destruction cycle items: fire, red, pointed

Flow of Fur Chi

As you can see there are items, colors, and shapes that can either be complementary (creating growth and a smooth flow) or not so complementary elements and items (causing weakness and blockage) that one can put into each of the elemental guas of the fur bagua. In Fur Shui the same applies to places and activities.

Just how you ask? It is quite simple and fun to take a look into the bagua elements with their creation cycles and apply these to our furry friends. For example . . .

Water Supportive Cycle:

In the life path sector of the Fur Shui bagua, the element is water and the complement would be metal and the shape is irregular. Does this remind you of walking your pooch after his meal with lots of water and having him "dowse" all the fire hydrants (metal) in the hood? Water and walk may take you both in good health along the life path yellow brick road. Take a look at a typical water supportive cycle illustrated on the next page.

WATER

Water Supportive Cycle

Metal Supportive Cycle:

The creativity gua has the element of metal in it's home and the complementary element would be earth, with the color of yellow and the shape of flat or horizontal. This translates easily into supportive cycles in Fur Shui. Take your cat and your bird as complementary proof. There's the gold- or earth-toned birdseed on a flat, metal plate or on the bottom of the bird's metal cage. Earth feeds the bird and the bird remains safely protected by the flat, square metal grid. The bird can freely sing it's song for all to enjoy, even your cat that sits patiently, ever watchful from below. Forget to put in the earth and the bird will not sing. Remove the metal, and the cat becomes your only pet! Keep the metal strong and the earth abundant and just hear the creative flow of song and watch the tap tap tapping of furry tails to the beat.

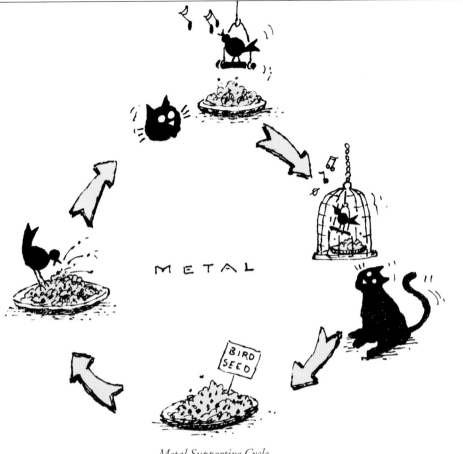

METAL

Metal Supportive Cycle

Fire Supportive Cycle:

Fame: This gua has the element of fire with a complement element of wood along with the color green and columnar shapes. There is nothing more comfortable or comforting for you and your furry friend as a burning hearth with your dog or kitty by your side or on your lap. You can start by putting more wood on the fire, starting up your kitty's engine with a few purr strokes and see how nice and comfortable an evening can be with your feline on top of those lap leg columns. As the wood burns down into soft glowing embers, you will still have the fire of your friend's love to keep you nice and warm. Deep long purrs and doggie soft snores make for strong supportive fire chi (along with loving groupie fur friends) to enter your Fur Shui fame sector.

FIRE

Fire Supportive Cycle

63

Wood Supportive Cycle:

Wood is the element of the gua representing family. This has its creation cycle complementary element of water with the shape being undulating and the color of black. Blackie the dog just loves to fetch the stick or wood you throw for him! This cycle keeps going only if you give him plenty of H_2O (and a few treats) to keep him running strong. Fetching plus drinking equals a very balanced and happy friend. You now have a loyal, happy, and healthy fur family member strengthening your Fur Shui family tree (If not also occasionally watering the trees too).

*Fur Shui Alert! *Paperboys and postal people, with their thrown papers and packages, are not to be considered fair game and are considered a no-chase zone for a fire supportive cycle. Only coconsenting tosses are allowed.

Wood Supportive Cycle

Earth Supportive Cycle:

Health is so important for you and your animal friends. The element of earth finds its home in the center of the fur bagua and is balanced by the element of fire along with the color red and pointed shapes. In the garden of Hawaii, the goddess Pele pours out lava creating new earth. In your own yard you can witness the fire of your dog (God spelled backward) creating new landscapes and valleys. Just give your pooch a bone and watch him fire up! He'll use the earth not only to plant his treasure, but also go prospecting deep into the dirt for his previously hidden treasures. Fire and earth become a healthy creation cycle for your dog, but could possibly be viewed by your gardener as a destructive cycle. In Fur Shui, you must breathe deeply (good for your health too) and just look at it as healthy aeration keeping your garden well turned and your dog fit and exercised.

Earth Supportive Cycle

The Other Side of Constructive

Now, the limiting (destructive) cycles are of a whole other nature. Sometimes you can use a limiting element to balance out an excess of an already present element. An overly excitable and energetic animal could have too much fire. You could introduce some more water, color, shape, element into its environment. When they get into balance, then take away the extra water element influence. Take some lessons from the previous Fur Shui creation cycles. It's a matter of balance, just enough of each element with its complementary elements, shapes, and colors. Be like the wise and pretty Goldilocks and make just the right choices for harmony and well-being or the world could become quite unbearable.

Too Much Water Element

An example from a Fur Shui wood limiting cycle would be the combo of the dog and the wood stick for fetching. Replace the wood stick with a metal one, and you will have no game at all and a possible emergency trip to the vet for teeth repair.

Another replacement of items in the creative cycle for water could be hazardous also for your good buddy,

the guy dog. Flatten all the fire hydrants and put in sharp, pointy wooden sticks and I believe your guy dog will have to find construction porta potties along your walk route.

Your purring and snuggling friends content by the fire would probably change their tune in Fur Shui if you installed a water fountain in the hearth and invited them in on a cold and stormy evening.

If destructive or limiting cycles are common in your animal or in your relationship with your friend, consult a professional to unearth some answers and guidance. An animal communicator (like me!) can put you in touch with your fur friends, ask some questions, and give you some clues and confidence in turning negatives into positives.

So, create via Fur Shui supportive cycles, keep it in the positive, and have a happy, healthy, balanced home and relationship with your animal friends. It is easy, joyous, and loads of fun!

Fur Shui Alert!   *When you apply a limiting element to balance out an excess of one or more elements, *always* remember to remove the limiting or controlling element after your friend has come into balance. If you don't, then you may have another issue with imbalance caused by the introduced element.

Too Much of a Chi Thing

As with anything in fur and nonfur life, too much of a good thing can be quite destructive. This is so true of the elements and their corresponding colors and shapes. Too much metal in Fur Shui can lead to taking your dog's breath away along with his creative urge to play and bring you joy. Too much water on your walk can be damaging to your overcoat, carpets, and entryway during your best friend's reentry shake down. Too much earth and digging can complete "the great escape" tunnel onto a busy street. Too much fire can result in loud territorial (Mexican, Persian, German, or *any* breed) standoffs causing emotional and possible physical trauma for you and your furry friends. Too much wood can give a woodchuck a tummy ache!

Try removing some of the element that is causing a disruption or blockage, then adding the opposite (chart on page 51) to cure and calm a furry situation that is out of sync or balance. Balance is the key for healthy, flowing, loving, and fun-filled Fur Shui days.

Fur Shui Alert! *Always consult an expert (vets, trainers, homeopathy MDs, chiropractors, acupuncturists, communicators, etc.) if you notice extreme behavior in any way physical or emotional. Lots of helpful people are out there who can come to the rescue if needed!

Fire + Fire = Combustion

The Body Language of Fur Shui

In Black Cat Fur Shui as in Black Hat Feng Shui body parts and pieces live in each and all the guas of the bagua. Take a bagua look at both your and your animal's body. See what is working or not in each gua and then put your imagination to work to create a better result or condition by enhancing, exercising, or healing your fur friend's particular parts and pieces.

Life Path/Career Gua:

Ear

Hear, hear, are we listening? Calling all ears, listen up and hear your purpose and life path calling. Your animal's ultrasharp hearing alerts you to take notice of opportunity knocking at your front door, or could be warning you of the exact opposite. So, protect and keep their hearing sound for your own good and their well-being.

Testing, One, Two, Chi

Helpful People/Travel Gua:

Head

If your head aches and your progress stalled out, take a break! From dreams to day tripping, keep alert, use your head, and find your way back home. When a horse breaks free it travels straight back to the barn where there is always shelter and a helpful person and some great food waiting. Common horse sense says: Get ahead by using your head. So, keep it strong and nimble by always walking the high roads. Helpful people, guardian angels (and animals), and of course adventurous dog walks and road trips with furry friends always come to the rescue.

Children/Creativity Gua:

Mouth

Look who's talking! Are you speaking your truths? Animals always speak their truths if you would *only* listen with your heart. Like children, teach them positive "speak" in beautiful tones and volumes, and happily accept their bright smiles. (Good reason to keep their teeth checked and cleaned often.)

What came first, the meow or the treat? Your fur friends chortle, purr, bark, coo—talking all the time. Watch what you say around that bird of yours, you may just find he finds creative ways to repeat your speak. All types of fur friends find creative ways to verbalize their needs and love from licks to carrying around security love blankies. And of course a Frisbee dog champ claims its fame with daring, one-of-a-kind aerial mouth snatches.

High Fly'n' Chi-Catch

Cooo-Chi, Cooo-Chi, Cooo

Love/Relationships Gua:

Heart

(The heart and all the major organs of the body.)

Just follow your heart and see how lovely life can be. Furry folk have strong loving hearts for you and each other. Just try to resist that cute little kitty, puppy, bunny, or baby bird. That's love and your heart talking to you!

Fame/Reputation Gua:

Eye
Look at me, look at me, eye can see you! Sharp eyes help with spotting that opportunity for fame (possibly an all-star mouser or maybe even a famous furry movie star) and pouncing on it.

"Loooook into My Eyes . . . "

Carnac the Cat

Hip

Hip, hip, hip hurray one must live a loving, joyous, and prosperous life. Go for a walk with your fur friend and get that chi a movin', keeping those hips groovin' for them and you. Hula lessons (with or without the hoop) are fun too!

Hip, Hip Fur–ray

Foot

Go ahead, put those feet firmly on the ground. Build good foundations by clipping those kitty and puppy nails ("petacures" are essential for pampering and health, check with your vet for timing). Horseshoes can be especially lucky when expertly fitted on a family of healthy hooves.

Foot Fit + Form = Fur Shui Auspicious Foundations

Skills/Knowledge Gua:

Hand
Black Hat Confucius says: "A skillful hand in life brings peace to the soul and much gold to the palm." Or a skillful swat in time nabs nine, or at least one mouse!

You may also need to employ the hand of a reputable trainer or behaviorist if things get a bit out of hand with your furry friends' actions or activities with you or others in your home.

The Hand Is Quicker than the Mouse

Health/Balance and Harmony Gua:

All the rest of the body not mentioned yet.
Putting it all together takes well-being, agility, and bodily coordination. When perfectly balanced, the body whole is greater than its parts. Keep this center gua clean and shining like a golden coin. Calling all body parts, all systems "gold," focus on balance . . . on your mark, get set, center!

Three Chi Cheers for Body Balance

Some Part Particulars:

Are there parts that need more attention, body parts that are overactive, parts that just plain bother your fur friends, or parts that just feel great? Amp up your home, or your pets' favorite places to strengthen or calm physical traits or symptoms. Obviously, if in need, bring in the Docs, along with the medics (both Western and Eastern). You could also spruce up the center of your home with the color gold (take a bit of gold paper and put your friend's name on it and place it here) if you are in need of good health in any area. Let's say if your animal is a bit nearsighted (like my one cat), you could put a nice comfy bed or pillow for him in the fame section (which would also help bring his natural fire energy to add to your fame) of your home. Or you might place a snappy red collar or ID tag around his neck!

If your bird stops singing and seems to be OK, if you can, place his or her cage in the creativity section of your home or get a new white cage for your chirping friend.

Maybe your friend is just home from the vet or is recuperating from an internal or external illness. Try placing his bed in the love gua or the health gua along with a yellow pillow or blanket. Amp up the healing!

Constant barking or howling . . . check out what's going on with the creativity section of your home. Maybe you have a destructive cycle, element, color, or shape in this area? Or you just may need to begin a creative cycle by more walks or doggie training classes.

Take another look at this section; be creative and find your own Fur Shui applications to stimulate or subdue activities in various furry body areas.

Take a Number Please!

There are also specific numbers and shapes (all from ancient feng shui practice) that represent each gua. Try these numbers and forms in their gua spaces to bring positive chi into your and your fur friend's home and life.

FUR SHUI NUMBERS AND SHAPES CHART

Gua	Number	Shape
Life Path/Career	6	Irregular, undulating, free form
Helpful People/Travel	5	Shape is anything that pleases you
Children/Creativity	3	Round or mounded shapes
Love/Relationships	2	Any shape is OK
Fame/Reputation	1	Pointed shapes or triangular
Wealth/Prosperity	8	Any shape goes, maybe a "$" shape?
Family/Elders/Community	4	Rectangular, vertical, columnar
Skills/Knowledge	7	Shapes are defined by your own tastes and skills
Health/Balance	9	Square, flat, and horizontal

Career:

#6/Irregular, undulating, free form

For animals that have careers (or make a career out of getting you to pamper them), six would be their best number! With their energy in your career sector along with the big six, you or they are bound to reap the rewards of realizing a strong life path or career.

Fido could spend hours (or even make a career out of) chewing on a variety of free-form bones, treats, and goodies lovingly placed at your entry door. Keep that six-noted wind chime undulating and free form with a nice catnip toy at the clapper strings' end. (A six-toed cat at the door could also spark that career chi.)

"Six-Noted" Career Salute

Helpful People and Travel:

#5/Shape is anything that pleases you

Give 'em the high five in your helpful people and travel gua. A super chi energizer for your helpful people gua could be your helpful friend's ability to fetch and hold five balls at once (and then teaching him or her to drop those balls into the play box when finished). Round, square, pointy, whatever shapes (especially five of them) you like are OK to attract all helpful things.

Five in One Gets a Chi High-Five

Creativity/Children:

#3/Round or mounded shapes

Three is *not* a crowd in the children, creativity section of your life or home. If your fur group (especially bunnies) is busy multiplying again, just stop at three not thirteen! Juggling many creative ideas at once? Try teaching your cat how to juggle a few round sparkle balls . . . hey, cats are swift of paw and tons more talented than they let you know. Three is better than one in this sector.

Two Hearts Fur-ever One

Love/Relationship:

#2/Any shape is OK

Where there are two, there is love. Back to the bunnies again (or birds, bees, kitties, and pups), it just takes two to make twenty-two. Pairs of like-minded things, items, souls are great in your and their relationship gua. All couples cuddling reinforce this gua, any shape or size is acceptable! That long weiner dog can be in love with that tall, svelte whippet. All types of pairs here; feline/canine friendly and inseparable pairs, dogs that carry about their stuffed teddy bears, and of course a furry friend that lovingly cuddles up to its person.

Fame/Reputation:

#1/Pointed shapes or triangular

All for one and one for all! The big number one lives in the fame sector. Being number one draws not only admiration but also fame. Your number one friend in this sector adds flame to that fame. Make your fur friend's bed into a royal throne graced with a large pointed star. Maybe a kitty pyramid tent bed in this gua? A nice star ID tag for a fur friend's star status? Or, take your dog to the ball game along with that big "#1" pointed-finger mitt. He and you could become famous on the giant screen during the seventh inning stretch. Go Sox!

#8/Any shape goes, maybe a $ shape?

Eight is the number of the gua holding your prosperity and abundance. The figure eight when laid on its side stands for infinity. To attract that infinite amount of wealth and prosperity place a photo of eight goldfish in this corner. This is also the place for those frogs with coins in their mouths (explained later). Why not try one facing into your room sitting atop eight pieces of eight? Round coins (good for tossing and swatting about), rectangular hundred-dollar bills (rubbed with catnip!), a pile of irregularly shaped yummy bones (dog booty), all can attract uplifting Fur Chi into this gua!

Family/Elders/Community:

#4/Rectangular, vertical, columnar

Four makes a powerful supportive foundation in the family sector. Four legs make for a very solid, steady foundation. Fur animals just naturally have it with number four. A tall kitty condo here will certainly benefit and attract your kitty family to this section. (Good place for the kitty box also . . . as long as it is kept sparkling clean!)

Fur Shui Four on the Floor

Skills/Knowledge:

#7/Shapes are defined by your own tastes and skills

Seven is at home in the skills and knowledge gua. Teach Fido or Fluffy a few skillful tricks or jobs and reward 'em with seven treats. Success and reward live here with lucky seven. Whatever shape you like for those treats is fine for this gua: tube chew sticks, fish-shaped yummies, triangle, square, round, or even people-shaped (mailman and police treat people are popular) goodies.

Health/Balance and Harmony:

#9/Square, flat, and horizontal

Nine is sublime for the health center of your bagua. To add balance and harmony, place a special healthy treat for your sweet feline here to augment its nine lives. Shapes are square, flat, and horizontal. A square gold or yellow neck kerchief for Rover will help him balance.

A soft, flat, square cushion (maybe even a soothing massage?) for rest and relaxation here will give a boost to their health and yours.

Nine Lives Ener-chi-zer

Beyond Fur Shui (Nonfurry Bringers of Fortune)

Bagua frogs, turtles and fish, oh my!

Ancient Chinese had a few or more auspicious animals that are known as keepers of good fortune, prosperity catalysts, and protectors. Many people are not able to keep furry folk because of allergies, housing restrictions, footloose travel, career choices, or spouse and family health issues. Not to worry, you can always have one of these animals (or any animal for that fact) in carved, painted, or sculpted form (please no stuffed real critters, OK?). And then, lots of people have both their live furry folk along with these carved critters inside and outside their home, all attracting luck, protection, and downright beauty. Let's just touch on a few animals, real and mythical, that can be kept easily without walking, feeding, or cleaning up after.

Turtles are linked to wisdom, long life, great fortune, and prosperity, as well as protecting your good fortune. Turtles are mentioned in the wealth section for bringing good fortune. Live turtles are great and pretty easy to keep healthy and happy in your home. A small carved turtle in your pocketbook or as a statue in your wealth sector can be just as effective at bringing in good luck and protection. Little carved jade turtles can bring great luck in wealth if worn in bracelets, amulets, or sitting on your car's dash if you are a traveling consultant. A chain of eight turtles yields much luck and wealth.

Money Chi Talks

Frogs have a lot to do with luck, wealth, and abundance. Replicas of these creatures are most likely holding Chinese coins in their mouths. Sometimes two frogs will be sharing coins, facing each other, holding an edge of the same coin between their lips. Place these coin-laden frogs in your abundance or wealth corner in your home or office. Rules on frogs: always place the frog facing *inside* and not outside (money then goes outta your house or business). Put these amphibians only in your living room or dining room or office space. Both frogs and fish are never to be placed in kitchens, baths, or bedrooms (your prosperity goes down the drain)!

Fish are known to bring luck and good fortune also. Those koi ponds in Asian gardens are peaceful, beautiful, and filled with good luck—alive and prosperous. Carved fish can frolic at your homes' entryway (where water is the element) bringing much good chi into the home. Fish are mentioned in the career gua section, having a nice place at an office entrance to bring in lots of lucky chi to your career and business transactions. Step into the Mirage casino in Las Vegas next time you are on the strip and be greeted by the huge, clean, beautiful aquarium tank filled with colorful fish. Abundance, money, wealth: come on in and spend!

A few other famous animals are known in the Far East to have qualities worth our while. One of those is the foo dog. They look a lot like the pug dog of today. This special dog is a fierce sentinel for both people and property. Pairs are common symbols of protection, just like some of our real dog (pugs especially) friends. They come carved in stone, wood, and formed in highly decorated ceramic. Most of the time you find these foo dog types in pairs guarding the outside doors of homes, offices, and places of business, one on each side of the door or opening. Man's best friend, the foo dog pair!

Dragons live in the East and are thought to bring great luck and prosperity. They are usually found in the fame or wealth section of the home along the east side of the property.

"Puff"-Shui!

They often live alongside the tiger (mostly *white* tigers) that act as your protectors. Tigers and dragons can be carved of wood or stone, painted on canvas, or adorn beautiful ceramics. They typically are placed outside the office or home front doors as guards (who knows, maybe it could turn its claws and fangs against you). According to intent in Black Hat Feng Shui and Black Cat Fur Shui, if you are attracted to tigers (as well as to any animal), if they are your totem or guide, then you will feel comfortable placing this ferocious cat inside your office (or other areas of your home). Domesticated cats, tigers or not, can really bungle up your computer intake fan and wipe out your work in progress by running over your keyboard. They can also play many games like find the paper clip in the paper piles, scattering your filing system to all points of the compass. So, it's a wise idea to keep all cats, live or carved, on the outside as ferocious guards at all times.

There are many inanimate animals (i.e., phoenix, roosters, mandarin ducks, three-legged frogs, etc.) that could augment your various guas, home, and life. But, let's get back to the animated typical furry friends, what they can do for you and what you can do for them.

Fur Shui Scents and Sounds

Smells are *oh* so important for Fur Shui. Your kitty rubs up against the walls and your legs to say hello and put his mark on you, saying, "I love you so, you are mine!" Smell is how your pooch meets and greets others at the local hydrant and doggie park. A good way to use *your* powerful chi here is to let your animal have an old T-shirt of yours (of course; not freshly washed) to cuddle up against in your partnership corner (the pink relationship gua in your home) if you are gone overnight or on vacation. Put something of yours in that traveling crate going to and from the vet to calm your animals down and reassure them you are always with them. Dogs and cats that try to fit their whole body into your shoes are just showing you they love to love you, love to smell you!

Furry friends respond to a whole list of aromatherapies that can help them remain cool and calm during change, emotional and physical upset, or loneliness. Look into it with an expert in the field for definitive aroma solutions. Let's look at some practical applications of some household aromas that bring in positive chi to some of the bagua areas.

Scent-imental Fur Shui

✍The wafting scent of baking turkey into the health sector will have both feline and canine friends begging for your attention, while cracking open that sardine can in this section will most likely be satisfying for the kitties in your company.

✍The scent of a fresh outdoor breeze can calm and enchant any fur person, so much that they may just jump for joy in your career entrance bagua stirring up all sorts of good chi for both you and them.

✍Stop and smell the roses (or any kind of flower!) in the relationship section of your home. Sweet fragrant smells of success here for your relationships both furry and nonfurry. There's nothing like the fresh scent of lavender (not for cats . . . be careful) in your dogs' bed that helps soothe them into their beauty rest and sweet dreams.

✍Who doesn't (furry and nonfurry) enjoy the nice smell of burning oak or hickory in a well-stoked fire in the fame section? Watch the fame sparks fly! Warm, furry, and friendly for that spot.

✍Mandarin oranges are known to represent abundance and bring great wealth. Animals also feel abundantly calm and happy when a nice orange scent is coming from the wealth sector of your home. Watch them smile as they charge up your wealth sector.

95

Tidy Chi Is Happy Chi

On another note, not so great smells can chase the chi right out of your and your pets' habitat. A messy, smelly kitty box (and most likely *outside* the box, "revenge chi") is a sure killer of chi for all. So, keep that spot neat, clean, and well ventilated. You may want to place this in your helpful people area. By keeping the box both clean and neat you help your kitties stay healthy and they help you by relieving themselves only in the litter box. A relief to all of you, all helping each other!

Sounds are also important to you and your fur friends. In Fur Shui, a nice, soothing melody playing by their bed in the health sector supports their health and sleep. Please, no heavy metal, jarring rap, or loud polka tunes here. Reports show that classical music increases the IQ. Played in the skills and knowledge gua can become a background for you all during those tricks and fetch classes you could be conducting.

Animals can hear noises that we cannot, and many are bothersome and hurtful to their sensitive ears. Sharp high notes, sirens, and horn blasts can send them running and that means their wonderful chi goes, too. Leave the air horns to the fire department. And, no sharp claps (practice on that bugle or drum set downstairs only and give your animals and neighbors a big break!) around the family gua, or your furry friend will depart the family tree. Please, just nice words, soft sounds, and nice melodies only on the old homestead.

Continual Fur Shui Blessings!
ommm mani padme hummmmmm
(ohm mah-nee pahd-mee hum)

Blessings! You now have a bit more understanding of chi, the bagua, and some universal energies that affect your and your fur friends' space, health, and life. I leave you with the above Tibetan mantra (calling loving forces to bring harmony, peace, and deep compassion into your life). It is an ancient blessing that is used in placing wonderful positive intent, loving kindness, and compassion on one's efforts or plans. Say it out loud and you will receive its blessings for you and your fur friends as you are planning and putting the proper elements, colors, shapes, sounds, and smells into your homes, activities, spaces, and places (even on your furry friends' bodies . . . get out those bagua-colored collars, leashes, toys, and cages).

In Black Cat Fur Shui as in Black Cat Feng Shui: what you think is what you get! So by all means keep it positive and be very aware of *how* you are thinking. Doing all things Fur Shui from placements to actions without the *belief* that things will strengthen, change, or grow will just not get you the results you are working to receive. Black Cat says: "Do the work, then let go of the outcome." This means just that . . . pay attention, be aware, charge up your fur person's life, and then believe it is already done!

Fur Shui principles can augment your furry and nonfurry relationships, life paths, travel, creativity, skills, family unity, fame, and fortunes *if* and only *if* your activities are focused and in constant alignment with your free will. Have you ever seen Fido start out chasing your thrown stick, spot a strolling kitty, then veer off course completely forgetting the stick, and *you* end up chasing him? It all turns out well though, giving you both the unexpected advantage of extra exercise. Showing you that once you change your focus, your results and timing will also change.

Animals as well as people have free will. Being an animal communicator has given me the opportunity to see the truth in this fact. Animals *choose* to be with you. They also choose their jobs, and fulfill their purposes. They know what your free will has chosen, react to it, and consequently respond to *your* choices. Another reason to watch what you think . . . they know what you are thinking even before you say the words. Many animals get lost because they feel they are not being given the opportunity to do their life path jobs. Watch your animals closely; do they hang out in your relationship area tying to help you into or out of a partnership? Or are they telling you to pay more attention to loving and caring for them? Are they curled up in your prosperity or fame corner as you wait for that job assignment or pay raise (adding some extra chi to get things moving)?

Becoming aware of the chi coming from and around your fur friends will make you more aware of their needs and yours to make major or subtle changes that can benefit all of you. Use Fur Shui to change and improve many aspects of your friend's life, from physical comfort to emotional support and compassion.

Black Cat also says If you act to change something, embrace the change and the form in which the change comes. Put the wish into the relationship gua for a cute little furry loving companion (listing color, sex, breed, etc.) and you get a rather large furry but loving friend who does not quite fit your original idea. Accept it, love it, and you will certainly receive even more than the ton of love you set out to receive. The Fur Shui universe responds to your *needs*. So, keep your thoughts focused and positive and go with the flow of chi coming your way.

Much gratitude for bringing your attention to Fur Shui and the fun romp into the fur bagua. Many blessings to your efforts in moving some fur chi in positive ways to show your deep love and appreciation to all fur friends. All furry folk give constant unconditional love, joy, support, and loyalty to their people; it is only natural that we find ways to bring fun, joy, and peace into their lives also. I hope Fur Shui brings you much fun, love, and many positive days!

Fur Finis (Blessings and Namastes)

Many heart-filled thanks I give to all the people who have encouraged, corrected, laughed with me, and believed in this effort. *Thank you* to my friends, teachers, and even to my loving skeptics.

My heart belongs to the many animals and their people that I have had good fortune to help. Without these communication experiences, my life would not be as deep or complete. Thank you for letting me be the conduit and messenger of the pleasures of your animal's expressions of love, frustration, fulfillments, struggles, and joy. You have been my main inspiration and encouragement to put together *Fur Shui*.

To my many animals past and present that have acted as "ghost" writers and insistent taskmasters for this effort. Rocky the rockstar cat sitting at my computer desk showing disapproval when I was not at work on *Fur Shui*, and his deep loving purr while I worked on each page. And, Boomer the bear cat's fetching of many kitty toy gifts, placing them on my lap with loud meows of encouragement and endorsements. Thank you from the depths of my heart for your unconditional love and joy!

May the Wise Black Cat Star Guide and Shine upon You!

About the Author

Paula Brown is an animal communicator as well as feng shui practitioner. She combines energetic alternative solutions with her telepathic communications, using the principles found in Feng Shui and other modalities.

Her communication studies include being a student and graduate of Carol Gurney; worldwide known animal communicator, lecturer, teacher, and author. Study with Monty Roberts; the original horse whisperer, and "listening" to nature with The Flower Essence Society rounds out her communication education. Along with the success from Brown's own communications practice, The Heart of Conversation (Bird in Hand), she takes referrals from around the world.

She graduated from both The Black Hat School of the Tibetan/Hawaiian Institute of Feng Shui, and the Qi Gong program at Emperor's College of Traditional Oriental Medicine. She has been a guest lecturer for holistic and alternative healing organizations, taught animal communications workshops, and has been written up in various news media including the San Diego Union Tribune featuring holistic alternatives for animals and pets.

Paula's Web site is www.animalhearttalk.com.

Fur Shui is the write stuff

Furr
Shui
Purr
Shui
Purr
Shui
Purr
Shui
Purr
Purr
Purr
Purr
Purr
Purr
Purr
Purr